SEASON OF CAROLS
for SOLO CELLO and PIANO

SONG TITLE	PIANO ACCOMPANIMENT	SOLO CELLO
Deck The Hall	4	1
Away In A Manger	6	2
Greensleeves	8	3
God Rest Ye Merry, Gentlemen	11	4
O Come, All Ye Faithful	15	6
Silent Night	18	7
Ding Dong! Merrily On High!	21	8
Chanukah, Oy Chanukah	25	10
Pat-A-Pan	29	12
O Holy Night	32	13
Three Holiday Songs	35	14
We Wish You A Merry Christmas	40	16

ISBN 978-1-4234-2625-7

HAL•LEONARD®
CORPORATION
7777 W. BLUEMOUND RD. P.O. BOX 13819 MILWAUKEE, WI 53213

Visit Hal Leonard Online at
www.halleonard.com

FORWARD AND PERFORMANCE NOTES

The idea behind the creation of these arrangements is to provide music that would be performable by student musicians who have studied string instruments for at least one year. Equally important is to provide interesting high quality arrangements of popular traditional holiday songs with a level of musical sophistication not often found in student literature. This effort has resulted in material that could be programmed by professional players as well.

Each piece has challenges which align with studies and techniques a student player encounters in popular second and third year string educational programs.

• FINGERINGS
The vast majority of the violin parts can be performed in 1st position, if needed. I have marked many 1st position fingerings as helpful reminders for the student and as aids to the teacher. At times a passage may require shifts to other positions, or be more playable in other positions, so I have given optional notes for 1st position playing where necessary.

• BOWINGS
The bowings have been marked as a starting point, and to a certain extent, take into consideration the young students' lesser bow control. There are, of course, other possibilities for bowings depending on the ability of the players and the desired musical result.

• POSSIBILITIES FOR PEDAGOGY
All of these pieces contain the opportunity to explore dynamics. They also have harmonic content that is a bit sophisticated and, in that way, can be opportunities to focus on intonation.

Away In A Manger: Legato bowing; bow control.

Deck The Hall: Playing off the string, playing marcato.

Ding Dong! Merrily On High!: "Bell Tones" *fp*; staccato; intonation.

Greensleeves: Many optional positions; legato bowing; expression; balance.

God Rest Ye Merry, Gentlemen: Tempo changes; off the string; optional double bow strokes.

O Come, All Ye Faithful: Tonalization; dynamics.

Chanukah, Oy Chanukah: Easy optional double stops; bowing.

O Holy Night: Bowing; simple duplets in 6/8; slightly chromatic harmony.

Pat-A-Pan: Probably the most challenging piece in the collection; open string pizzicato; key of G minor introduces "lo 1" fingering for B♭ and E♭; key change to A minor.

Silent Night: Bow control.

Three Holiday Songs: Pizzicato section can be bowed if desired.

We Wish You A Merry Christmas: "Bell tones" *fp*; key change from G major to D major.

I'd especially like to thank Gail Acosta, David Killen and Nancy Schindler for kindly reviewing the pieces and making helpful suggestions.

Bruce Healey

SEASON OF CAROLS is also available for:

Solo Violin and Piano....00841986

Solo Viola and Piano......00842194

String Quartet..................04490404

String Orchestra

Conductor....04490308	Violin 3 (opt.)....04490311	Piano......................04490315
Violin 1.........04490309	Viola..................04490312	Harp (opt.)..............04490316
Violin 2........ 04490310	String Bass.........04490314	Percussion (opt.)....04490317

DECK THE HALL

Traditional Welsh Carol
Arranged by BRUCE HEALEY

AWAY IN A MANGER

Words by JOHN T. McFARLAND (v.3)
Music by JAMES R. MURRAY
Arranged by BRUCE HEALEY

GREENSLEEVES

16th Century Traditional English
Arranged by BRUCE HEALEY

GOD REST YE MERRY, GENTLEMEN

19th Century English Carol
Arranged by BRUCE HEALEY

O COME, ALL YE FAITHFUL
(Adeste Fideles)

Music by JOHN FRANCIS WADE
Latin Words translated by FREDERICK OAKELEY
Arranged by BRUCE HEALEY

00842195

16

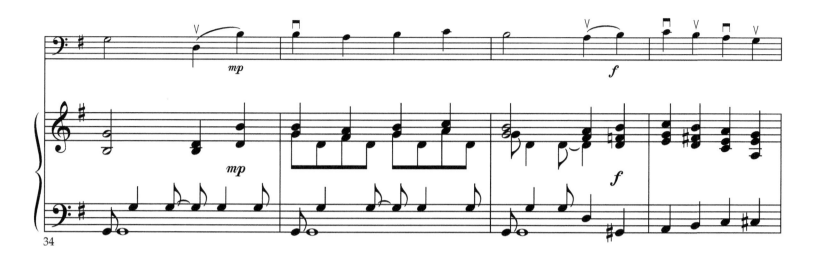

SILENT NIGHT

Words by JOSEPH MOHR
Translated by JOHN F. YOUNG
Music by FRANZ X. GRUBER
Arranged by BRUCE HEALEY

DING DONG! MERRILY ON HIGH!

French Carol
Arranged by BRUCE HEALEY

00842195

CHANUKAH, OY CHANUKAH

Traditional Hebrew Lyrics
Chanukah Melody
Arranged by BRUCE HEALEY

26

PAT-A-PAN
(Willie, Take Your Little Drum)

Words and Music by BERNARD de la MONNOYE
Arranged by BRUCE HEALEY

O HOLY NIGHT

French Words by PLACIDE CAPPEAU
English Words by JOHN S. DWIGHT
Music by ADOLPHE ADAM
Arranged by BRUCE HEALEY

THREE HOLIDAY SONGS
(The Dreydl Song • Jingle Bells • Joy To The World)

Arranged by BRUCE HEALEY

"The Dreydl Song"
Traditional

00842195

23 "Jingle Bells"
Words and Music by J. PIERPONT

"Joy To The World"
Words by ISAAC WATTS
Music by GEORGE FRIDERIC HANDEL

4th pos.

1st pos.

WE WISH YOU A MERRY CHRISTMAS

Traditional English Folksong
Arranged by BRUCE HEALEY

42

00842195